ALBERTA
HIGHLIGHTS

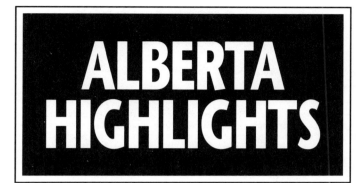

Linda Hall & Diane Webber

Pine Candle Adult New Reader's Series

PINE
CANDLE

Copyright 1991 by Alberta Association for Adult Literacy
Printed in Canada
First printed in 1991 5 4 3 2 1

The publisher:
Lone Pine Publishing
206, 10426-81 Avenue
Edmonton, Alberta, Canada
T6E 1X5

Canadian Cataloguing in Publication Data
Webber, Diane.
   Alberta highlights

ISBN 1-55105-004-8
   1. Readers for new literates.   2. English language — Textbooks for second language learners.
3. Readers (Adult)   4. Alberta — Description and travel — 1981-   I. Hall, Linda, 1950-   II. Title.

PE1126.N43W4   1991   428.6'2   C91-091628-4

Cover illustration: *Horst H. Krause*
Editorial: *Lloyd Dick*
Printing: *Kromar Printing Ltd., Winnipeg, Manitoba, Canada*

The revision of this publication was made possible by a grant from the Secretary of State for the International Literacy Year (1990).

The publisher gratefully acknowledges the assistance of the Federal Department of Communications, Alberta Culture and Multiculturalism, the Canada Council, and the Alberta Foundation for the Arts in the production of this book

Photo Credits:
Alberta Tourism - pp.10-11; p.12; p.24; p.54; p.56; p.57
Rick Hall - p.14.
Calgary Olympic Development Association - p.16.
Calgary Zoo - pp.20-21.
Royal Tyrrell Museum of Palaentology - p.23; p.26; pp.28-29.
Muttart Conservatory - p.30.
West Edmonton Mall - pp.32-33.
Fort Edmonton Park - pp.36-37.
Fort McMurray Oil Sands Interpretive Centre - p.39; p.40.
Nikka Yoko Japanes Garden - p.44; p.46.
St. Paul Chamber of Commerce - p.49.
Holiday Photo - Vegreville - p.50.
Lesser Slave Lake Provincial Park - p.58.
Cypress Hills Provincial Park - pp.60-61.

THE LAST TEN YEARS

Finding suitable and enjoyable reading material for adults reading at basic levels has always been a problem. In 1980, literacy instructors at Lakeland College in northern Alberta decided to produce the books they needed themselves. Literacy instructor Colleen Hanley received a summer STEP grant and hired two people, Diane Webber and Terri Fuglem, who wrote and illustrated the original 13 booklets over two summers. The ideas for the booklets came out of brainstorming sessions between Colleen, Terri and Diane. "I had a pretty good idea of my student's interests," said Colleen.

Copies were sold to and used by numerous literacy programs throughout Alberta. In 1984, the Alberta Association for Adult Literacy took over the copyright. Colleen, an AAAL board member at the time, felt that a provincial literacy association would be better than a college at selling books.

In 1990, the AAAL received an International Literacy Year grant to revise, rewrite and upgrade the six most popular booklets in the series. Literacy instructors and students were polled as to their favourites. Linda Hall was hired as editor for the AAAL. Lone Pine Publishing was contracted to edit, produce and market the new books. A lot of research, revising and updating was done.

The Pine Candle Adult New Reader's Series is the result. With the co-operation of Lone Pine Publishing, we have produced a series of six books that can be read and enjoyed by the "adult new reader." But many other people should also find them enjoyable, useful and informative.

There are six books in the Pine Candle Adult New Reader's Series:

Alberta Highlights
Helpful Home Hints
Hockey: Canada's National Game
Night Skies
Rodeo West
Souped Up

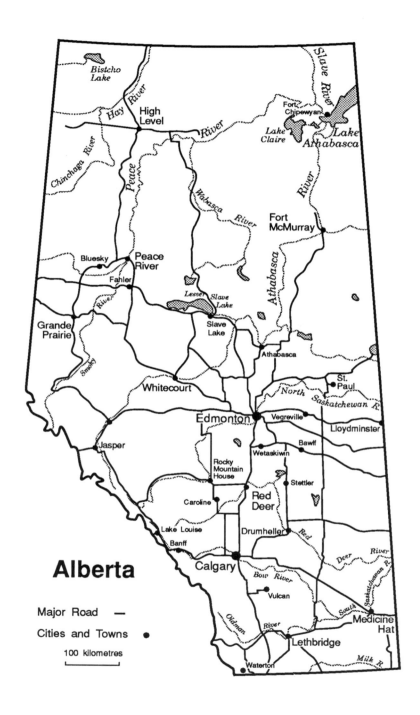

Bistcho
Lake

Slave River

Hay River

High
Level

River

Fort
Chipewyan

Chinchaga River

Peace River

Lake
Claire

Lake
Athabasca

River

Wabasca River

Fort
McMurray

Athabasca

Bluesky

Peace
River

Fahler

Lesser Slave Lake

River

Slave
Lake

Grande
Prairie

Athabasca

Smoky

St.
Paul

Whitecourt

North Saskatchewan R.

Edmonton

Vegreville

Lloydminster

Jasper

Bawlf

Wetaskiwin

Rocky
Mountain
House

Stettler

Caroline

Red
Deer

Lake Louise

Drumheller

Red

Banff

Alberta

Calgary

Deer River

Bow River

Vulcan

Saskatchewan R.

Major Road —

Cities and Towns ●

Oldman River

South

Medicine
Hat

Lethbridge

100 kilometres

Waterton

Milk R.

ALBERTA
A FEW FACTS

Alberta, Canada's most western prairie province, was named for Princess Louise Caroline Alberta. She was the fourth daughter of Queen Victoria. Lake Louise, in the Rocky Mountains, was named after this princess. The town of Caroline, near Rocky Mountain House, was also named for her. Alberta became a province on September 1, 1905.

More than two million people (2,429,200) live in Alberta now. That sounds like a lot. Yet there are more than 26 million people in Canada. Alberta has just 10 per cent of Canada's population.

Alberta's landscape is more varied than any other province's. In the north there is farmland, forest, and muskeg. Muskeg is like swamp land. Many people farm in the north. The long summer days help crops grow well there. Others in the north work on oil rigs or in lumber camps.

Central Alberta is park land. Park land is a mixture of flat prairies, rolling hills, and a few forests. Central Alberta is also one of the best farming spots in Canada. Southern Alberta is pure prairie. Ranches and farms give a good life to the people there.

Lake Louise, Banff National Park.

In the west are the Rocky Mountains. They separate part of Alberta from part of British Columbia. They are some of the most dazzling sights in North America. Mount Columbia is Alberta's highest mountain. It is 3,747 metres high. The highest peak in all of the Rockies is Mount Robson in British Columbia. It is 3,954 metres high.

Alberta has 245 rivers. It also has 315 creeks and 600 lakes. That sounds like a lot of water, but it only takes up one per cent of Alberta's land.

Alberta is well known for its chinook winds. They blow across the south in the winter. A chinook is like a bath of warm air. The warm winds seem to spill down from the Rockies. A chinook can sometimes raise the temperature more than 25 degrees in just one hour.

The city of Edmonton.

People know about the Calgary Stampede, the West Edmonton Mall, and skiing in Banff and Jasper. But did you know that Alberta has a UFO landing pad? And that Alberta also has the world's largest Easter egg, and one of the world's littlest airport?

Read on to discover what else Alberta has....

BAWLF
ALBERTA'S LITTLEST AIRPORT

There is a very different kind of airport just 22 kilometres east of Camrose on Highway 13. It is the best airport of its kind in North America. The key words are "of its kind."

The planes which land at this airport weigh only four to eight kilograms. You can hold one in your hand. Are you curious?

Bawlf is an airport for radio-controlled planes. The pilots fly their planes using radio transmitters which they hold in their hands. The radio sends signals to the plane in the air. The pilots can steer their planes and make them move up and down. They can make them loop, spin, dive, and, if they're not careful, crash! Alberta's Littlest Airport is one of the most advanced in the world. There are many runways. It looks just like a full sized airport, only in miniature.

This airport has one of the biggest competitions for radio controlled planes in North America. During the summer they also have weekend "Fun Flies." These weekends are good chances for people to get together and look at each other's planes.

There are many "fun flies" during the summer at Bawlf.

BLUESKY
HOME OF THE DOLLAR

For about 20 years, whenever Bluesky residents wanted to show someone a picture of their town, all they had to do was to reach into their wallets. Between 1954 and 1973 the farming town of Bluesky was pictured on the dollar bill. After 1973 that was changed. A picture of the Parliament buildings replaced the peaceful Bluesky skyline.

The people of Bluesky like to point out that after their picture was removed from the bill, the value of the Canadian dollar fell below the U.S. dollar.

To remind people that Bluesky was once had its picture in everybody's wallets, the town would like to build the biggest dollar bill in the country, complete with the original picture of Bluesky.

CALGARY
DEVONIAN GARDENS

There is a large garden right in downtown Calgary, and it's 14 metres up off the ground! On the fourth floor of the Toronto Dominion Building is a lush paradise. It is a one hectare garden park. A 1.6 kilometre path winds through 20,000 plants. But that's not all. There are wooden bridges, sparkling fountains, waterfalls, colourful birds, and two gardens with seats for 800 people.

The top of the 90 metre ski jump is higher than any building in Calgary.

The garden also has a play area for children. In winter, one of the pools is turned into a skating rink. There are stores and restaurants all around. It is a great place to shop. It's also a very popular place for wedding pictures.

HERITAGE PARK

Heritage Park is Canada's largest historical village. It has 100 restored buildings on 26.7 hectares of land. The entire area is set up like a town in the early 1900s. At Heritage Park you can go for a ride on an antique steam engine. You can ride on the S.S. Moyie, a sternwheeler boat. You can also watch demonstrations of old farming methods and shop in old village stores.

CANADA OLYMPIC PARK

The 1988 Winter Olympics were held in Calgary. The people of Calgary went all out. They even kept their Christmas lights on until the Olympics were over.

Calgary is keeping the memory of the Olympics alive. You can visit the place where the Olympics were held. Sometimes you can even watch athletes training for future Olympics. You can ride a chair lift to the very top of the ski jump tower. The top of the 90-metre ski jump tower is higher than any building in Calgary.

You can ride on the same luge run that the athletes raced on. But you will ride the lower 450 metres of the track. You can travel as fast as 45 kilometres per hour. Guiding a sled with your feet and lying on your back may sound dangerous, but it is actually quite safe.

If you are more daring, you can ride the bobsled. This ride goes more than 100 kilometres per hour. But you won't ride it alone. Two members of Canada's bobsled team will go with you. After your ride is over you will get your picture taken with a team member. You will also receive a special pin to help you remember your ride.

If you are not quite so daring, you can take a ride on the ski jump simulator. It feels as if you are skiing, but you are actually standing still on a platform. The pictures on the screen in front of you give you the feeling that you are actually skiing down the ramp, and then making a spectacular jump. The crowd even cheers when you land!

The Canadian Olympic Hall of Fame is at Canada Olympic Park. Canadian medal winners from past Olympics are honoured there. The displays always change. There is always something different to see.

CALGARY ZOO

More than 1,400 animals live on an island in the middle of the Bow River. The island is St. George's Island. The animals are part of the Calgary Zoo. You can visit the zoo

Modern elephants walk with the giants of the past at the Calgary Zoo.

all year round and see grizzly bears, gorillas, leopards, elephants, and much more. There are 315 different species of animals there. The Calgary Zoo is one of the largest zoos in Canada. It is world famous.

The zoo opened in 1920. The first animals to live there were two mule deer, two turtles, and a swan. Since that time, hundreds of animals have come to live in the zoo. The animals in the zoo are happy and well cared for. They are not kept in cages. They roam around in large spaces.

The Calgary Zoo has a prehistoric park with models of full-sized dinosaurs. You can walk through the park, which looks like Alberta may have looked a million years ago. You can see models of lush swamplands, volcanoes, ancient oceans, and hoodoos. Hoodoos are thick pillars of hard, white sand. Flat stones or chunks of earth sit on top of these pillars. Hoodoos are formed by erosion. Wind and water carve them out of deep beds of hardened sand. "Hoodoo" was an Indian word which meant "a person or thing that brings bad luck." The Indians thought hoodoos were men made of rock, who came alive at night and threw rocks at people passing by.

The Calgary Zoo also has a botanical garden. There are colourful flowers from all over the world there. For example, there are dozens of kinds of orchids in the Orchid Garden. Many of these orchids are endangered species. They come from tropical forests which are in danger of being destroyed.

In the Butterfly Garden you will be able to see how insects are important to plants. In some cases, they cannot survive without each other.

DRUMHELLER
THE ROYAL TYRRELL MUSEUM OF PALAEONTOLOGY

Dinosaurs ruled the earth for 120 million years. The last ones died millions of years ago. Today they live only in books and in museums like the Tyrrell Museum in Drumheller. Walking through the Tyrrell Museum is like stepping back in time.

The Tyrrell Museum is named for Joseph Burr Tyrrell, a geologist. Geologists study the layers of rock under the surface of the Earth. More than a hundred years ago

The Royal Tyrrell Museum of Palaentology, Drumheller, Alberta.

Hoodoos are thick pillars of hard, white sand. You can see models of hoodoos at the Calgary Zoo. These natural hoodoos are in Drumheller, Alberta.

The *Edmontosaurus.*

Tyrrell studied the rocks near Drumheller. He found a 70 million-year-old dinosaur skeleton. He called it *Albertosaurus*.

In the Tyrrell Museum you can meet some other members of the *Saurus* family. Meet *Brontosaurus*. It is also known as the "thunder lizard." The ground shook under its 30,000 kilograms when it walked. It would take seven large elephants to total 30,000 kilograms. *Brontosaurus* was 21 metres long. Luckily for the other dinosaurs, it just ate plants.

Then there was *Tyrannosaurus*, the "king" of the dinosaurs. It stood six metres high and was 13 metres long. Some of its teeth were 12 centimetres long. It could kill any animal with its jaws.

Next is *Stegosaurus*, a walking tank. It had two brains. The one in its head worked the front half of its body. The other brain was near its hips and worked its legs and spiked tail. Bony plates covered this reptile. A dangerous spike, often used as a weapon, grew on its tail.

The *Edmontosaurus* had a mouth that looked like a duck's bill. It weighed four tons and had a long, flat tail. This reptile had more teeth that it knew what to do with. A thousand teeth filled its jaws.

The Tyrrell Museum has the largest collection of dinosaur skeletons in the world. There are 35 complete dinosaur skeletons on display.

The Tyrannosaurus.

THE MUTTART CONSERVATORY

You may have seen pictures of the pyramids in Egypt. Edmonton has pyramids, too. In Egypt the pyramids are tombs. Edmonton's pyramids are not for the dead. Instead, they are places of life. All kinds of plants grow in these pyramids. Your senses of sight, sound, and smell will come alive there. The Muttart Conservatory has more than 700 kinds of plants and flowers in four glass pyramids.

THE ARID PYRAMID

"Arid" means dry. This pyramid looks like a desert. It is hot and dry and full of sand. This pyramid has desert plants. There are many kinds of cactus plants here. Some look like tall candles. Some look old and white-haired. Some have nice soft flowers. There are also many succulent plants here, as well. The leaves of succulent plants are filled with fluid.

The Muttart Conservatory, Edmonton.

THE TROPICAL PYRAMID

The tropics are the hottest places on earth. They are also the wettest and the greenest. The world's jungles are found in the tropics. This pyramid looks and feels just like the tropics. Coffee plants, rubber plants, vanilla plants, and ginger plants grow here. You will see all sorts of colourful ferns and orchids.

THE TEMPERATE PYRAMID

Temperate climates have both hot and cold seasons. Alberta has a temperate climate. Plants in this pyramid need to rest in winter in order to bloom in the spring. The temperate pyramid has the most plants. You can see plants from Australia, Asia, and North America here.

THE SHOW PYRAMID

This pyramid changes all the time. Flower shows mark the change of each season. The display of poinsettias at Christmas is wonderful to see. The autumn display of chrysanthemums is outstanding. But winter is the best. It is pure heaven to be surrounded by flowers when it is -30° C outside.

WEST EDMONTON MALL

Do people in Edmonton like to shop? It would seem so. Edmonton has the most retail shopping space per capita in all of Canada. Per capita means for each person.

West Edmonton Mall

The West Edmonton Mall.

Edmonton also has the largest shopping mall in the world, the West Edmonton Mall. Of course you can shop there, but you can also swim, golf, ice skate, watch a dolphin show, ride a roller coaster, and take a ride in a submarine.

The water slides in the World Waterpark are some of the largest in the world. If you like to swim in water with waves, you will enjoy the Blue Thunder wave pool. A special machine makes waves which are two metres high. There are 12.3 million litres of water in the pool. That's more than in some small lakes.

There are also real submarines in the mall. A ride in one of the mall's submarines will take you underwater to see animals and plants which live in all the oceans of the world.

And, of course, no visit would be complete without a trip to Fantasyland. The triple-loop Mindbender roller coaster is 14 storeys high. It goes very fast, and turns you upside down twice during the ride!

THE PROVINCIAL MUSEUM

Who were the first settlers in Alberta? How did they spend their days? What kind of houses did they live in? What kind of animals live in Alberta? All of these questions can be answered by a trip to the Provincial Museum of Alberta, in Edmonton.

One of the rooms or galleries at the museum features human history. In that room you will discover who first settled Alberta. You can walk inside of store fronts, which are exact replicas of ones that actually existed a long time ago. You can see the kinds of things that people bought and used then. You can see the kinds of machinery that people used on their farms.

In another display, you will learn about Alberta's native peoples. There are many artifacts and works of art from native culture on display. An artifact is an object made by people and used long ago. You will also find out about the main religions in Alberta, and how they added to the history and culture of the province.

In yet another gallery you will walk past displays of animals. Some of these animals lived in Alberta millions of years ago. Some of these animals live here now.

The Provincial Museum of Alberta opened on Canada's birthday, in 1967. Since then, many hundreds of thousands of people have visited it.

FORT EDMONTON

One of the first English explorers to come to central Alberta was Anthony Henday, in the 1700s. He was a smuggler. He was outlawed from England. The Hudson Bay Company, Canada's largest fur trading company, sent Henday to central Alberta. They wanted him to get

Fort Edmonton.

the fur trade going. He canoed up and down the North Saskatchewan River trading with Cree Indian trappers. He traded guns and other supplies for their furs.

In 1754, he spent the winter in Edmonton. In 1795, the Hudson Bay Company and the Northwest Company built a fortified fur trading post at Henday's campsite. Fort Edmonton was the main fur trading centre in the West. It was built and rebuilt many times. Finally, in 1830, it was rebuilt for the last time. It was constructed on the present site of the Alberta Legislature building.

Fort Edmonton Park is not right on top of the Legislature building today, however. The fort's buildings have been moved to the south side of the city. At Fort Edmonton Park, you can walk through the reconstructed fur trading post. You can see what Edmonton looked like in the early days.

FALHER
HONEY CAPITAL OF CANADA

Falher has about 1,200 people. It looks like a nice average small town. Look again. There are also 35,000 beehives here. Each year these hives produce more than two million kilograms of honey.

There are many different kinds of honey. Some taste strong and heavy. Others are very light and sweet. The taste of honey depends on which flowers the bees feed on. In Falher the bees feed on clover flowers. Many people think that honey made from clover flowers is the best quality. Most of the beekeepers in Falher ship their honey to Eastern Canada and Japan.

FORT MCMURRAY
OIL SANDS INTERPRETIVE CENTRE

The biggest deposits of oil sands in the world are right here in Alberta. Oil sands are sands which are mixed with oil. The oil is called bitumen. For a long time, this oil stayed in the ground because people didn't know how to separate the oil from the sand. Then in 1967, a new separation process was perfected. Mining soon began in Fort McMurray.

The Oil Sands Interpretive Center.

The lands around the Oil Sands Interpretive Center.

The deposits of oil sands are below the surface of the earth. Above them is a layer of earth and muskeg. That top layer must be scraped off first. Then, special chemicals are used to remove the sand from the bitumen. Then the crude oil travels down a pipeline to Edmonton. It is refined in Edmonton.

At the Oil Sands Interpretive Centre in Fort McMurray, you will discover how modern technology is used in this process. There is a viewing area where you can watch the sands being mined at Suncor, Inc. You can also take a tour of the Syncrude plant. On these tours you will get a chance to see the operation first hand.

GRANDE PRAIRIE
KLESKUN HILLS GEOLOGICAL PARK

There used to be a giant sea just north of Grande Prairie. Now it is just a wide expanse of dry land. On this ancient sea bottom are fossils of ancient marine life. Recently, scientists have found remains of *Hadrosaurus* there. It was a flat-headed duck-billed dinosaur. This dinosaur had very large eyes and a highly developed sense of smell. Visitors to this area can find out more about these ancient animals.

THE TRUMPETER SWANS

The trumpeter swan is the biggest waterfowl in the world. And Grande Prairie has the largest flock of trumpeter swans in Canada. Each spring these swans fly to Grande Prairie to nest and breed. They always return to the same nests. They just repair them with reeds and grasses. In the fall, after the cygnets, or baby swans, are hatched, the swans fly south to the hot springs in the Yellowstone National Park in the United States.

Before 1930, trumpeter swans were in danger of becoming extinct. A large conservation program began. Now the population of trumpeter swans is up to 8,000.

LETHBRIDGE
NIKKA YUKO JAPANESE GARDEN

Nikka Yuko means "Japan—Canada Friendship." Many Japanese people settled near Lethbridge in the early 1900s. The Nikka Yuko Garden was built in 1967 to honour the good feelings between Japan and Canada. A Japanese garden pleases your eyes. It also charms your heart. It is a place to relax in peace, a place where time stands still.

A gardener from Japan designed the four-acre garden. Japanese artists came to Lethbridge. They wanted to set

This friendship bell is a gift to Canada from the people of Japan.

up the garden correctly. Each rock and tree was picked and placed by hand.

Water is the first focus of this garden. Then come the rocks and stones. The rocks are placed in groups of three, five, or seven. Those are lucky numbers for the Japanese. The rocks suggest many things. They might be mountains, or they might be islands in a sea of sand.

There are no flowers in a Japanese garden. The Japanese believe bright colours can tire your eyes. Shades of green are much more restful. Trees, shrubs, hills, and ponds make up the rest of the garden. Even the paths are restful. They curve gently. Sharp corners are distracting.

There are six viewing areas in the garden. The first is the Pavilion, a traditional Japanese building. The Japanese tea ceremony is held in the Pavilion. The Dry Garden is like a garden inside of a garden. The white walls of the Dry Garden shut out every distraction. In this garden you can kneel on a wooden deck and admire the arrangements of white rocks.

The Azumaya, a traditional Japanese shelter, is another viewpoint. From it you can watch the stream rush across white pebbles. You also have a good view of the islands, the bell tower, the bridges, and the lake.

The Friendship Bell is in the Bell Tower. The bell was made in Japan. There is an inscription on the bell which says that Japan and Canada will always be friends. When the bell rings, it reminds everyone of this friendship.

The Nikka Yuko Japanese Garden

The Flat Garden combines the Japanese garden style and the prairie setting. From the Flat Garden you have a good view of the lake. There are islands in the streams and lake. Many of these small islands are shaped like turtles. The turtle is the Japanese symbol for long life.

The Nikka Yuko Japanese Garden opened July 14, 1967.. Since 1967, almost a million people have visited the garden.

ST. PAUL
THE ONLY UFO LANDING PAD IN THE WORLD

In 1967, Canada turned 100 years old. The town of St. Paul gave Canada an unusual birthday present. The gift was a UFO landing pad. UFO means Unidentified Flying

Provincial flags surround the UFO landing pad.

Object. The St. Paul landing pad is a place for flying saucers and space ships to land. St. Paul has the only UFO landing pad in the world.

The landing pad is 12 metres across and has a flat place on top for space ships to land. Canada's provincial flags are displayed all around it. A locked capsule was placed inside the pad. Letters in the capsule talk about life up to 1967. The capsule will be opened on June 3, 2067. Then Canada will be 200 years old. Will life change as much as it did during Canada's first 100 years? Will anyone have landed on the pad by that time?

VEGREVILLE
THE WORLD'S LARGEST PYSANKA

A pysanka is a Ukrainian Easter egg. Painting eggs is a Ukrainian custom. Ukrainians also decorate eggs for weddings and other events. They decorate eggs for good luck. Most of these pysankas are real works of art.

PYSANKA FACTS

		Number of pieces	
Total weight	1,350 kilograms	Sides	3,152
Lenght	7.75 metres	Nuts and bolts	6,978
Width	5.75 metres	Star patterns	524
		Triangular patterns	2,208

The people of Vegreville built a giant pysanka. They built it to say thank you to the Royal Canadian Mounted Police. The RCMP brought peace and helped to unite the people of the area.

Dr. Ron Resch used a computer to design the Vegreville egg. It took him one year to complete it. His design had to show the local culture. It also had to honour the RCMP. It is actually a giant jigsaw puzzle of triangles and star patterns. In the wind it acts like a weather vane.

The designs on this pysanka stand for many things. The gold stars stand for life and good luck. The pointed stars stand for the Trinity - the Ukrainians have a strong faith in God. The silver bands near the centre have no beginning and no end. They stand for eternity. Teeth point

Vegreville has the world's largest Easter egg.

from the bands to the centre. These stand for the protection and security that the RCMP bring. The three colours, gold, silver, and bronze stand for success. In the central section, gold and silver windmills with six vanes each mean a good harvest.

VULCAN
ALBERTA'S *STAR TREK* TOWN

There is a town in Alberta called Vulcan. It is an ordinary farming community in southern Alberta. Vulcan is also the name of a planet on the television series *Star Trek*. The people in Vulcan, Alberta are just ordinary people. They don't have pointed ears or fly around in space ships, like *Star Trek* Vulcans. But soon Vulcan won't look very ordinary. The people there want to build a huge model of the starship *Enterprise*, from the TV show. They would like to hang it above their grain elevators.

The people of Vulcan, Alberta sell Star Trek t-shirts and trinkets in their stores. The local newspaper has pointed Vulcan ears in its masthead.

The fictional planet Vulcan is famous for "grain-bearing grass." That is a staple on the planet Vulcan. Vulcan, Alberta is also known for its grain farming. It has 11 grain elevators. That's a lot for a small town. It is the world's largest primary grain shipping point. More grain is shipped out of Vulcan than from any other place in Canada.

NATIONAL PARKS
BANFF: CANADA'S FIRST NATIONAL PARK

In 1883, two railway workers saw a cloud of steam rising from the mountains near Banff. It smelled a little like eggs boiling. One worker walked to the place where the steam was coming from and found a very warm spring. It gushed out of rock. It was warm enough to have a hot bath in. They had just discovered the world's highest and hottest hot springs. These springs gush from rocks 1500 metres above sea level. The water is 45 °C.

A lot of different people wanted to claim the property the hot springs were on as their own. Finally, the Canadian government decided that the land should be preserved for all Canadians to enjoy. In 1887, Banff National Park was set up. It was the country's first national park. It was set up to preserve the hot springs and the wildlife in the area.

Banff has some of the most breathtaking scenery in all of Canada. Besides the hot springs there are hundreds of campsites near Banff. They are nestled in beautiful tree-filled settings near lakes, streams, and waterfalls.

In 1907, Jasper National Park was set up. Jasper is known for its glaciers, wildlife, and high mountain peaks. The highway from Banff to Jasper is called the Icefields Parkway. The view is simply spectacular. There are huge glaciers along the way. A glacier is a thick sheet of ice which does not melt in the summer. You can even climb on the Athabasca Glacier. That glacier is receding. That means it is slowly melting. There are sign posts which will tell you where the glacier was at different points in history.

The mountains are some of the most rugged in the Rocky Mountains. The Athabasca Falls are spectacular. There are many viewing areas all along the falls. As well, there are campsites and picnic areas along the way where you can rest and enjoy the scenery.

The Columbia Icefields.

Moraine Lake, Banff National Park.

WATERTON LAKES:
THE FIRST INTERNATIONAL PEACE PARK

Waterton Lakes National Park lies just north of the state of Montana. This park was set up in 1895. In 1932, the park joined with Glacier National Park in Montana. The park represents the peace between Canada and the United States.

As you drive toward the park you will notice that the watch herds of buffalo. The Red Rock Canyon is dramatic gorge of red rock carved by water. And you should not miss the Cameron Falls. They are a breathtaking sight to see.

Red Rock Canyon, Waterton Lakes National Park.

PROVINCIAL PARKS
LESSER SLAVE LAKE

Lesser Slave Lake is one of the largest lakes in Alberta. It is 90 kilometres long and 20 kilometres wide. It is a very shallow lake. It is only about 12 metres deep at its deepest point.

There are two provincial parks near the lake. At the Lesser Slave Lake Provincial Park there are very sandy beaches. The town of Slave Lake holds an annual sand castle building contest on Canada Day.

At the southern end of the park is a series of ancient beach ridges formed by glaciers. On Marten Mountain, near the park, is some rare plant life. Many of these plants are only found in the foothills region of Alberta. These plants are lodgepole pine and devil's club.

Devil's Club is a rare plant found near Lesser Slave Lake.

The Cypress Hills were missed by the Ice Age.

CYPRESS HILLS

These are sometimes called "the hills which shouldn't be." About a million years ago, huge sheets of ice spread south over much of North America. The ice came down from the north four times. Each time, it melted. All but the highest mountain peaks were a mile deep in ice. As the ice sheets slowly moved, they carried rocks as big as houses. They made small mountains even flatter. And they ground loose rocks into powder.

The melting ice formed huge rivers. The rivers carved out deep valleys where small streams are now. But there is one place which, for some reason, escaped the ice age. Now the Cypress Hills stand 1,400 metres above the prairie. They are like an oasis in the dry surrounding prairie. They are wetter and cooler than all the land around.

Plants and animals which are usually found in more southern areas are found in the Cypress Hills. There is a large population of wildlife, including 15 varieties of orchids. The park is an important archeological area as well. The remains of a 7,000 year old native camp have been discovered here.

The Cypress Hills Provincial Park is one of Canada's largest provincial parks. The area has many camping, picnic sites and hiking trails.

HISTORIC SITES
COCHRANE RANCHE

Alberta is known for its beef. But a little over 100 years ago, there wasn't any ranching in the area. Only buffalo roamed the prairie. In the late 1800s, Senator Matthew Cochrane decide to ranch in Alberta.

Cochrane was a successful rancher in Québec. He raised Shorthorn Hereford and Aberdeen-Angus cattle there. But he was intrigued by the West. He decided to take a trip there to see what it was like. He travelled through the United States and came north through Montana to Alberta. When he arrived at an area called Bill Hill (later renamed Cochrane in his honour), just west of Calgary, he decided to stay and set up a ranch.

He obtained 100,000 acres of land and then bought 6,000 cattle from Montana. His ranch hands wanted to drive the cattle north before winter came. They were unsuccessful. Most of the herd died along the way.

The same thing happened the next year. The cold winter killed half the herd before they could reach the ranch. The third year, Cochrane leased a tract of land much further south. But luck was not with him. That year, the old ranch site at Bill Hill was snow free while the new ranch site near Fort MacLeod had a cold and snowy winter. But Cochrane didn't give up. Eventually, he got cattle to the ranch and it prospered. The Cochrane ranch was the first large ranch in Alberta. It paved the way for other Alberta ranches, and Alberta soon boasted the best beef in the country.

The Cochrane Ranche has been a working ranch ever since. In 1977, it was declared a Provincial Historical Site. Now you can tour the Cochrane Ranche Historical Park. There are trails you can follow which wind through the ranch.

INDIAN BATTLE PARK

The Oldman River valley has been very important to the settlement of the Lethbridge area. In the early 1800s, the Blackfoot Indians (made up of the Blackfoot Blood and Peigan tribes) lived there. They called themselves the Prairie People. The Oldman River valley was their home. They looked at the seams of coal along the west bank of the river and called them "Sik-ooh-kotoks." This means "black rocks."

With that much coal in the area, it didn't take coal miners long to discover the Oldman River valley. The first coal miner came in 1874. His name was Nicholas Sheran. He began mining the small seams of coal along the river bank. His mining operation was very small, but it attracted the attention of another businessman, Elliot Galt. Galt developed Galt Enterprises, which set up large mines in the area. His mines operated until 1941.

In 1883, 35 miners came to work in the area. In 1909, construction of a Canadian Pacific Railway bridge over the river was completed. It was the longest and highest steel railway bridge in the world when it was built. It is 1,624 metres (5,327 feet) long and 97 metres (314 feet) high.

But coal isn't the only famous thing in the area. During the mid-1800s, two American traders, John Healy and Alfred Hamilton arrived in the Oldman River area. They set up Fort Whoop-Up. It was supposed to be a trading post for buffalo hides, but it soon became a centre for trading illegal whiskey. By 1874, the North West Mounted Police had been formed to stop the whiskey trade. They brought peace to the area.

In 1960, the Indian Battle Park opened. In Fort Whoop-Up, which is part of Indian Battle Park, you can see replicas of the original fort's buildings. You can examine artifacts from the era. You can even taste a bit of bannock after it is cooked over an open flame.